Big Machines on the Farm

by Brienna Rossiter

FOCUS READERS.

SCOUT

www.focusreaders.com

Focus Readers is distributed by North Star Editions:
sales@northstareditions.com | 888-417-0195

Produced for Focus Readers by Red Line Editorial.

Photographs ©: Shutterstock Images, cover, 1, 4, 7 (top), 7 (bottom), 9 (bottom), 11, 13, 15, 16 (top left), 16 (top right), 16 (bottom left), 16 (bottom right); iStockphoto, 9 (top)

Library of Congress Cataloging-in-Publication Data
Names: Rossiter, Brienna, author.
Title: Big machines on the farm / by Brienna Rossiter.
Description: Lake Elmo, MN : Focus Readers, [2021]. | Series: Big machines | Includes index. | Audience: Grades K-1.
Identifiers: LCCN 2020033608 (print) | LCCN 2020033609 (ebook) | ISBN 9781644936740 (hardcover) | ISBN 9781644937105 (paperback) | ISBN 9781644937822 (pdf) | ISBN 9781644937464 (ebook)
Subjects: LCSH: Agricultural machinery--Juvenile literature. | Farm equipment--Juvenile literature. | Farms--Juvenile literature.
Classification: LCC S675.25 .R67 2021 (print) | LCC S675.25 (ebook) | DDC 631.3/7--dc23
LC record available at https://lccn.loc.gov/2020033608
LC ebook record available at https://lccn.loc.gov/2020033609

Printed in the United States of America
Mankato, MN
012021

About the Author

Brienna Rossiter is a writer and editor who lives in Minnesota. She loves being outside and looking at stars.

Table of Contents

Tractors

A tractor plows a field.

It moves dirt.

It makes rows.

Tractors do many jobs.

A baler can help.

It packs hay.

It makes **bales**.

baler

bale

More Machines

A **planter** puts seeds in

the ground.

A truck fills the planter.

A tractor pulls it.

Sprinklers water plants.

They use long pipes.

They roll across fields.

sprinklers

Combines

A combine cuts grain.

A **reel** spins.

It pulls in plants.

reel

Grain comes out.

It comes from a **chute**.

It goes into a bin.